EMOTIONS and FEELINGS

Anger

Kari Jones

Explore other books at:
WWW.ENGAGEBOOKS.COM

VANCOUVER, B.C.

e WWW.ENGAGEBOOKS.COM

Anger: Level 1
Emotions and Feelings
Jones, Kari 1966 –
Text © 2023 Engage Books
Design © 2023 Engage Books

Edited by: Sarah Harvey
Edited by: Jared Siemens
Edited by: A.R. Roumanis
Design by: Rose Gowsell Pattison

Text set in Arial Regular.
Chapter headings set in Arial Black.

FIRST EDITION / FIRST PRINTING

LIBRARY AND ARCHIVES CANADA CATALOGUING IN PUBLICATION

Title: Anger / Kari Jones.
Names: Jones, Kari (Kari Lynne), 1966- author.

Description: Series statement: Emotions and feelings
Identifiers: Canadiana (print) 20230132448 | Canadiana (ebook) 20230134599
ISBN 978-1-77476-796-2 (hardcover)
ISBN 978-1-77476-797-9 (softcover)
ISBN 978-1-77476-798-6 (EPUB)
ISBN 978-1-77476-799-3 (PDF)
ISBN 978-1-77878-116-2 (Audio)

Subjects:
LCSH: Anger—Juvenile literature.
LCSH: Anger in children—Juvenile literature.

Classification: LCC BF723.A4 J66 2023 | DDC J152.4/7—DC23

This project has been made possible in part by the Government of Canada.

Canada 🍁

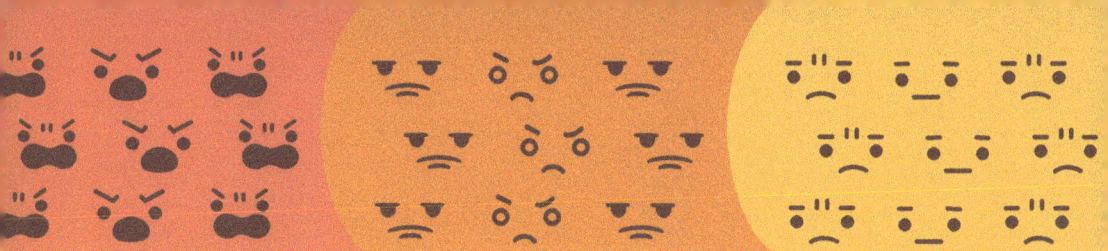

Contents

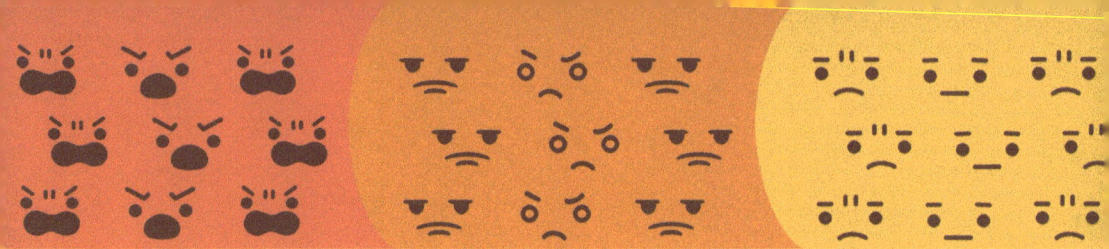

What Is Anger?

Anger is an **emotion**. It does not feel good. Many things can make you feel angry.

4

Something that makes you angry may not bother another person at all.

People get angry when they feel out of control.

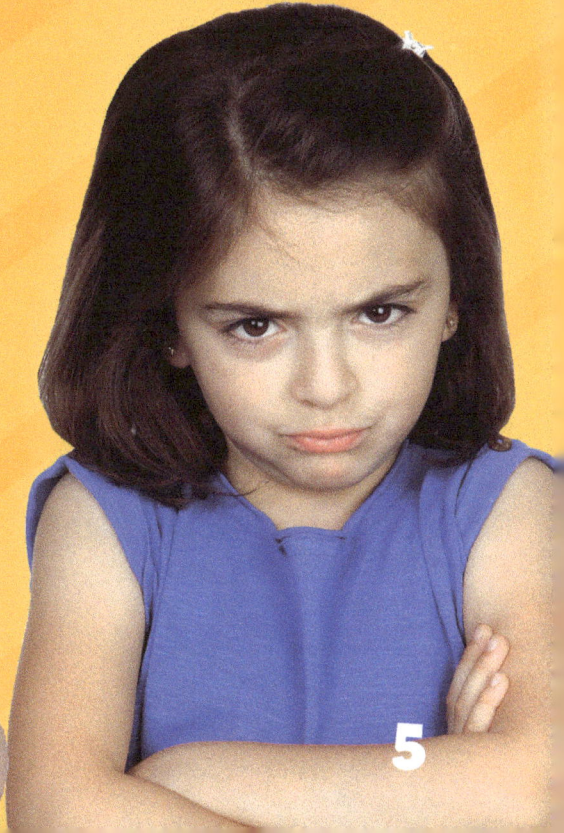

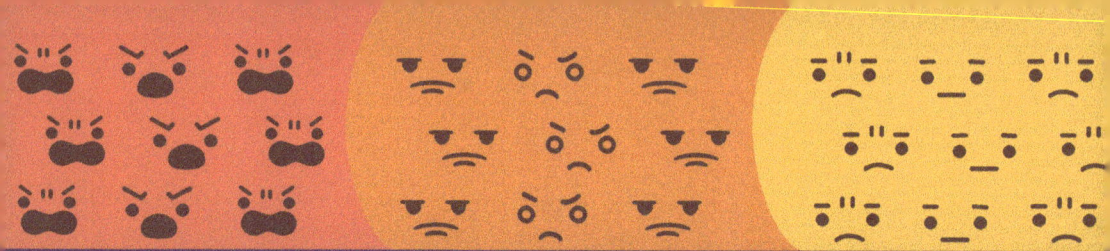

What Makes People Angry?

Being treated unfairly makes people angry. Not being listened to also makes people angry.

People get angry when they feel in danger. Getting hurt can also make people angry.

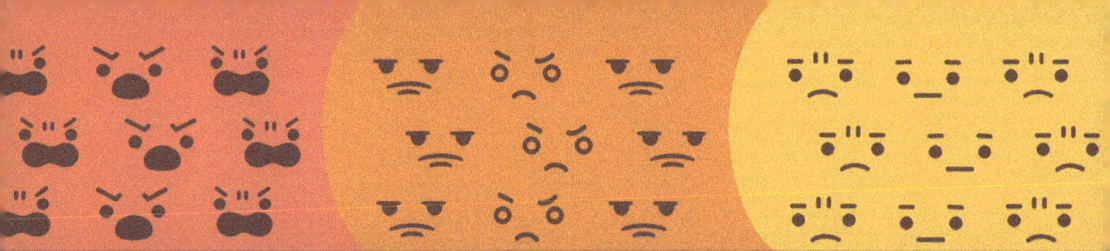

We often get angry
when we do not get
what we want.

Are There Different Kinds of Anger?

You might be a little angry if you do not get screen time. You might be much more angry if you are bullied.

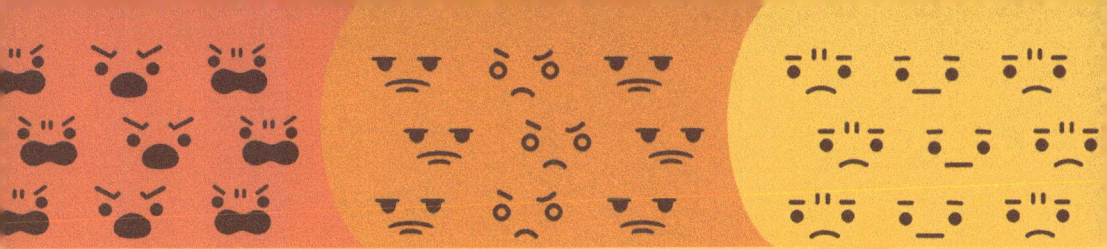

Some people get very angry and fight with others. It can cause problems in their lives.

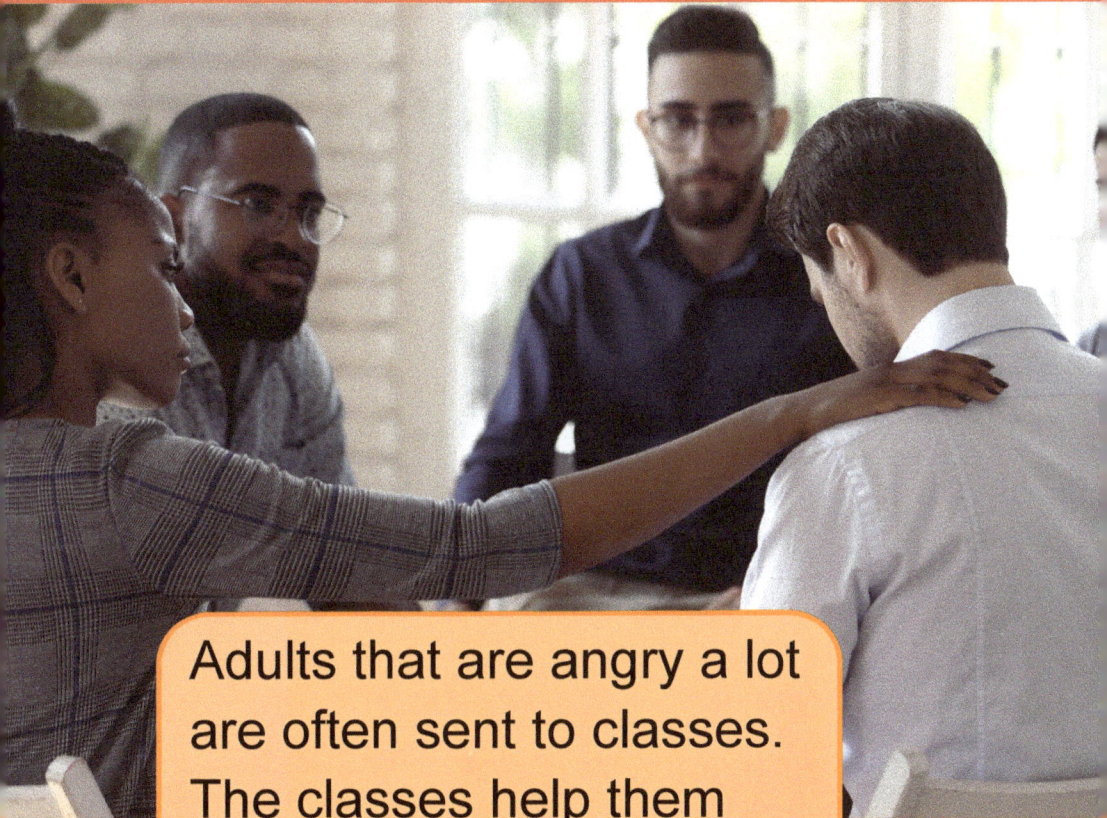

Adults that are angry a lot are often sent to classes. The classes help them control their anger.

9

How Does Anger Affect the Way You Think?

Anger can make us act without thinking. Anger can also make us feel guilt or **shame**.

KEY WORD

Shame: knowing that you have done something wrong.

Anger can also help you focus. It might make you want to try harder to learn something new.

How Does Anger Affect the Way You Act?

Seeing someone being bullied might make you angry. That anger could make you feel brave enough to help them.

Anger can also make us stay away from people. It's hard to be friendly when we are angry.

It can be hard to talk to people who are angry.

Does It Help to Know Why You Are Angry?

Knowing what makes you angry can help you deal with your feelings. Maybe you will be more aware when you start to feel angry.

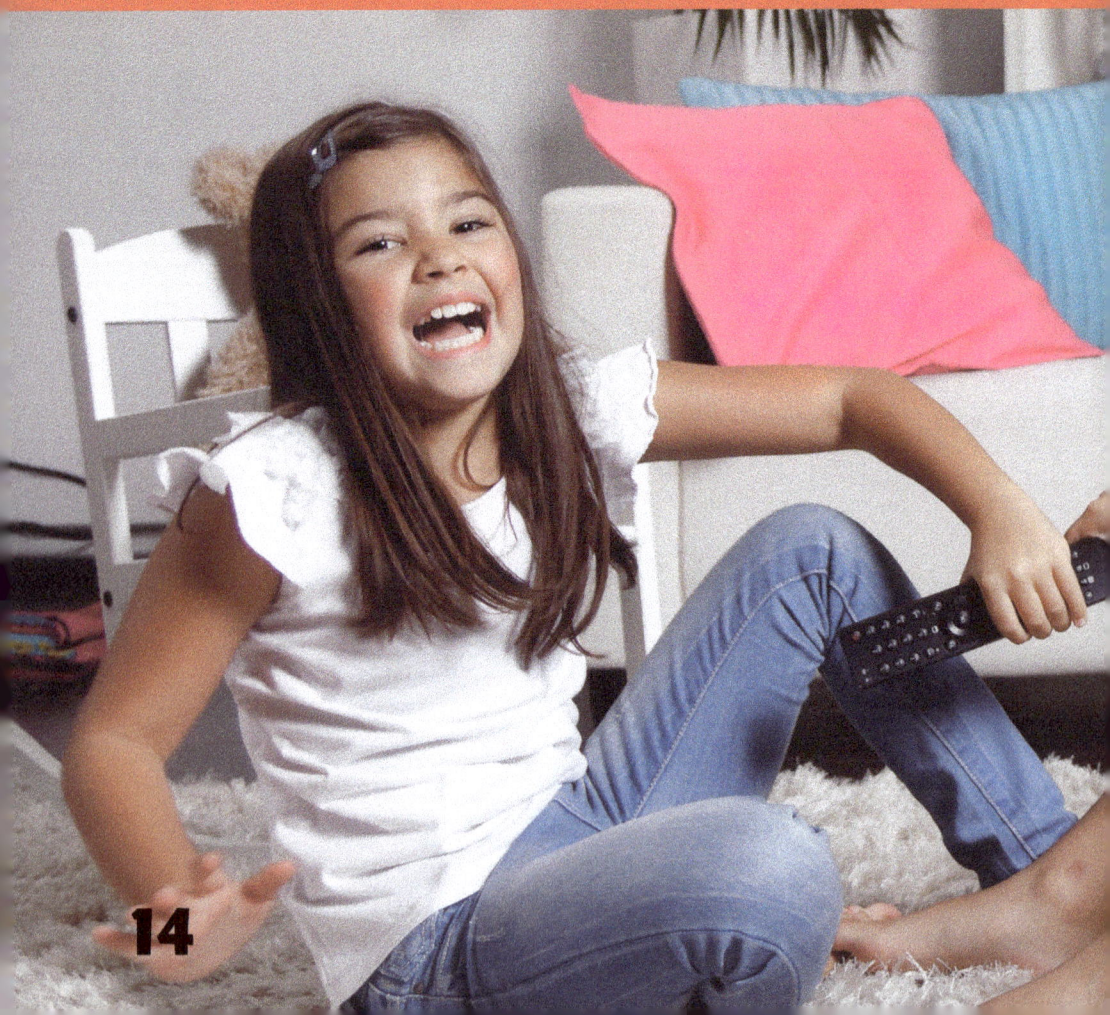

Most people try not to be angry. Too much anger can be bad for your health.

Children often get angry at their brothers and sisters.

Does Everyone Feel Anger?

Everyone feels angry sometimes. Some people get angry more often than others.

Some people show their anger. Other people hold it in.

Being tired makes you get angry more quickly.

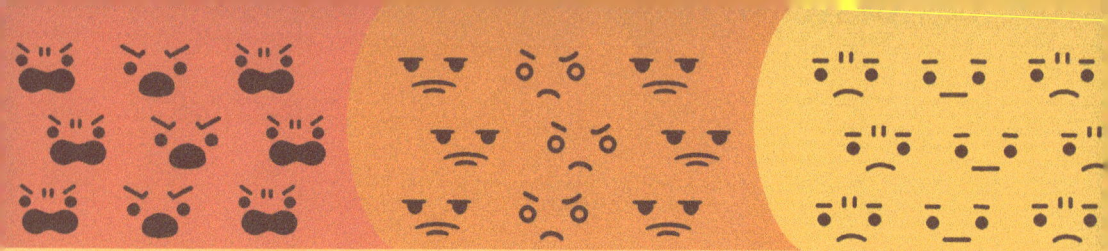

What Does Anger Look Like?

Some people punch or throw things when they are angry. Other people scream or cry.

Scientists think that dogs can help us stay calm when we are angry.

You might frown or close your eyes. It is okay to let yourself be angry.

What Does Anger Feel Like?

Your chest may feel tight when you are angry. Your stomach might also hurt.

Anger can make your heart race. Your hands might get sweaty.

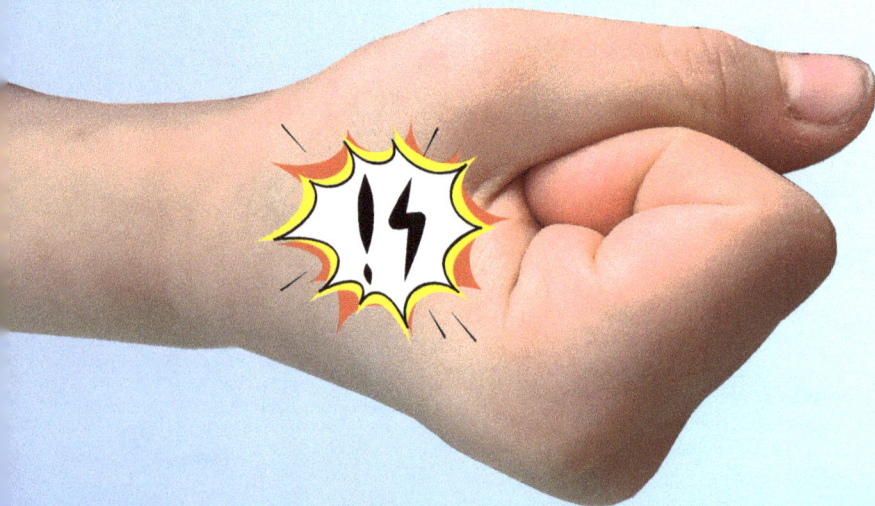

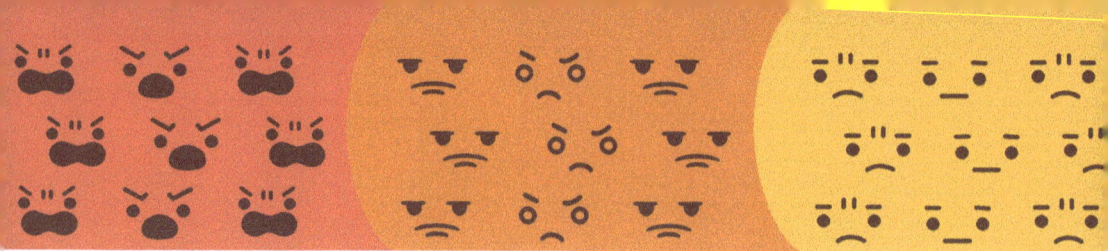

Can You Make Yourself Angry?

Failing at something can make you feel angry at yourself. You may also feel shame.

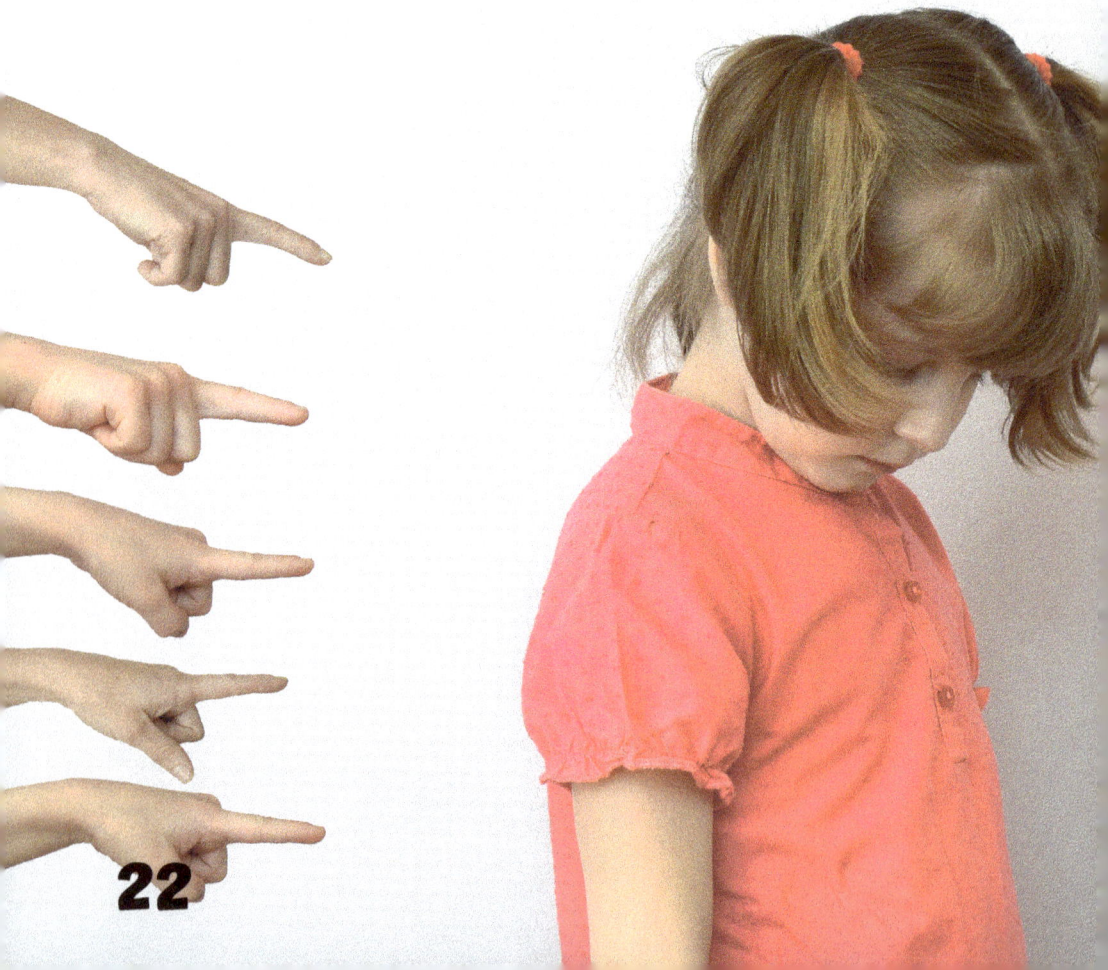

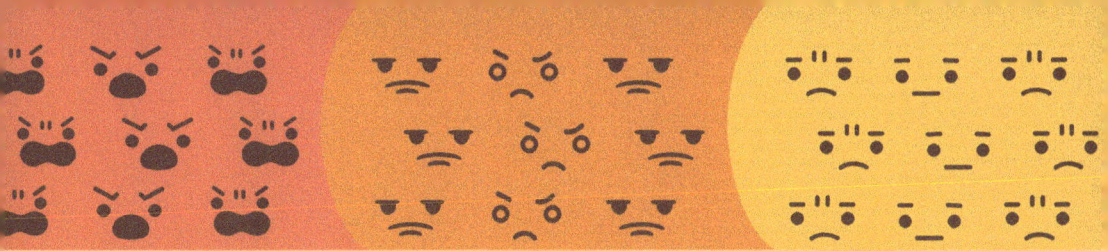

Breathing slowly and deeply can help when you feel angry. Ask an adult for help if you feel angry often.

"Where there is anger, there is always pain underneath."
– Eckhart Tolle

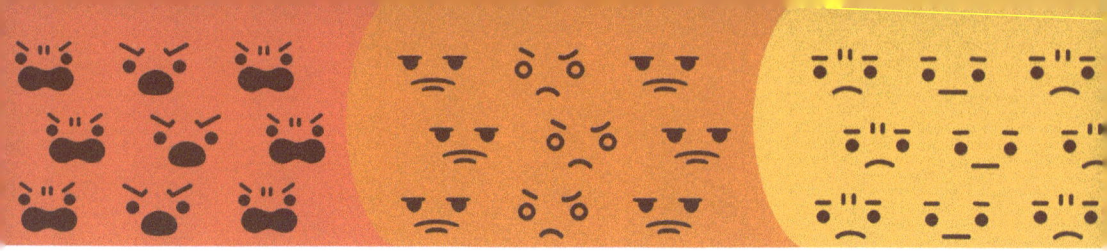

Can You Make Other People Angry?

People get angry if you are mean or rude to them. Leaving someone out can make them angry.

You can say sorry to a friend you made angry. Giving them time and space will help.

Does Anger Change as You Grow Older?

Most people learn to control their anger as they age. Little kids sometimes have **tantrums**.

KEY WORD
Tantrums: long, angry outbursts.

Going for a bike ride or a run can help calm you down.

Children often cry when they are angry. Adults might take deep breaths or take a time-out.

Can Anger Change the World?

A lot of kids are angry about **climate change**. Their anger leads them to speak out.

KEY WORD

Climate change: a change in Earth's temperature over a long period of time.

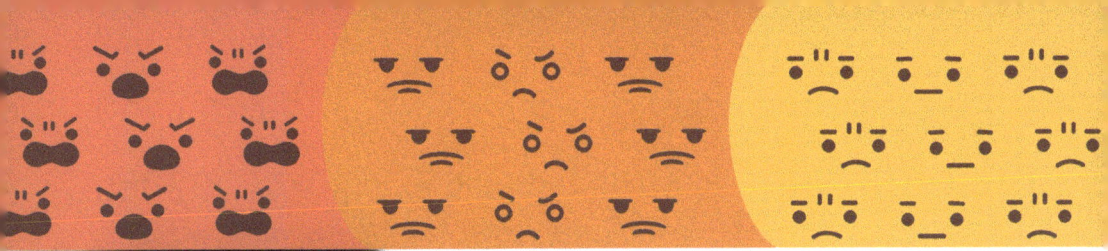

Being angry about unfairness is a good thing. This can lead to change.

"Sometimes, you have to get angry to get things done."
— Ang Lee

Quiz

Test your knowledge of anger by answering the following questions. The questions are based on what you have read in this book. The answers are listed on the bottom of the next page.

1 Does everyone get angry at the same things?

2 Can anger help you focus?

3 Is it easy to be friendly when we are angry?

4 Does everyone show anger the same way?

5 Can dogs help us stay calm?

6 Does being rude to people make them angry?

Explore other books in the Emotions and Feelings series.

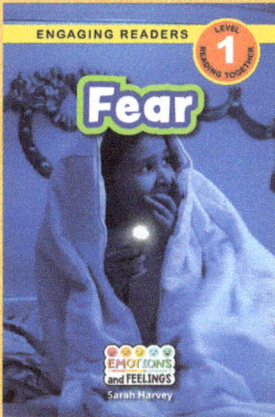

ENGAGING READERS — LEVEL 1 — Fear — EMOTIONS and FEELINGS — Sarah Harvey

ENGAGING READERS — LEVEL 1 — Happiness — EMOTIONS and FEELINGS — Kari Jones

ENGAGING READERS — LEVEL 1 — Sadness — EMOTIONS and FEELINGS — Sarah Harvey

ENGAGING READERS — LEVEL 1 — Surprise — EMOTIONS and FEELINGS — Kari Jones

ENGAGING READERS — LEVEL 2 — Gratitude — EMOTIONS and FEELINGS — Kari Jones

ENGAGING READERS — LEVEL 2 — Grief — EMOTIONS and FEELINGS — Sarah Harvey

ENGAGING READERS — LEVEL 2 — Guilt — EMOTIONS and FEELINGS — Sarah Harvey

ENGAGING READERS — LEVEL 2 — Love — EMOTIONS and FEELINGS — Kari Jones

ENGAGING READERS — LEVEL 2 — Worry — EMOTIONS and FEELINGS — Kari Jones

Visit www.engagebooks.com/readers

Answers:
1. No 2. Yes 3. No 4. No 5. Yes 6. Yes

www.ingramcontent.com/pod-product-compliance
Lightning Source LLC
Chambersburg PA
CBHW040226040426
42331CB00039B/3364